YOUR KNOWLEDGE HAS VALUE

AF130153

Bibliographic information published by the German National Library:

The German National Library lists this publication in the National Bibliography; detailed bibliographic data are available on the Internet at http://dnb.dnb.de .

Imprint:

Copyright © 2016 GRIN Verlag
Print and binding: Books on Demand GmbH, Norderstedt Germany
ISBN: 9783668766433

This book at GRIN:

https://www.grin.com/document/432920

Peter Sutor

Learning the Meaning of Nouns and Verbs. A Comparison from an Emergentist Perspective

GRIN Verlag

Universität zu Köln

Englisches Seminar II

Hauptseminar:

Lexical Disorders in EFL Classroom
SS 2013

Hausarbeit zum Thema:

Learning the Meaning of Nouns and Verbs:
A Comparison from an Emergentist Perspective

Verfasser:

Peter Sutor

Abgabe: 17.03.2016

Table of Contents

1. Introduction

Teachers of foreign languages have to face the question of how children learn languages in order to so organize their lessons und use such materials that the best possible learning results would be guaranteed. When thinking about these issues, they should be able to expect some help from professional researchers who are specialized in studying the psychological processes of language acquisition, learning and development from a scientific point of view. Every year an enormous quantity of literature on these issues is being published, so that – especially for a student who has to complete a vast array of courses in different subjects – it is simply impossible to keep track of even a substantial part of the latest developments in this area. Be it as it may, the student as well as the teacher have to start *somewhere* and try to grasp the theory as good as they can and then put this into use.

Unfortunately, there exist considerable gaps between the general theoretical orientations which are used by psycholinguists to study the psychological phenomena that involve language. Basically, to make the theoretical diversity somewhat simpler, it could be said that there are two general theoretical orientations among psycholinguists – the *nativists* and the *emergentists* or *constructivists*. The former assume that a considerable amount of linguistic knowledge in humans is pre-given biologically (Pinker, 1994, pp. 18-23). What is supposed to be genetically pre-wired is the knowledge of categories such as nouns, verbs or prepositions in terms of their syntactic properties, plus, some basic rules which regulate the combinatorial possibilities which, applied to these categories, allow the formation of larger linguistic units such as phrases and sentences. The emergentist approaches, on the other hand, assume very little innate knowledge structures on the part of humans, apart from rather general cognitive abilities like a certain capacity for memory or the ability to form concepts/categories, schemas or associations (Ellis, 1998; 2006; Bates et al., 1998). Putting this basic apparatus to use, they assume, languages can be learned.

These distinct theoretical orientations among psycholinguists have further consequences on how the processes of language learning are explained. One such consequence is that the *nativists* regard second language learning as being totally different from first language *acquisition* (cf. MacWhinney, 2006, p. 730). The reason for this supposition is the tenet that first language acquisition is the automatic unfolding of a putative *language acquisition device*, i.e. a biological program which controls the genetically pre-specified processes of language acquisition in young humans (Radford, 2004, pp. 5-9). At a certain age (when some kind of linguistic 'maturity' has been reached) the language acquisition device gives up its work and language learning becomes a very different process, based on general learning mechanisms (Pinker, 1994, pp. 290-296). Constructivists, in contrast, tend not to overemphasize the difference between first and second language learning/acquisition since both are considered to be the products of general cognitive functions like memory, categorization, schematization or association (Ellis, 2006). A second significant difference between the two theoretical frameworks is the 'nature' of grammatical categories such as nouns and verbs or prepositions. Whereas nativists assume them to be integral components of *universal grammar*, i.e. the linguistic knowledge structure which is produced by the *language acquisition device*, constructivists view categories as effects emerging from language use, without any fundamental or unchangeable cognitive architecture (Broccias, 2013, p. 198; Bybee & McClelland, 2007, p. 438). Besides, they believe that a word cannot be assigned any particular category per se, but that its category can only be determined within a syntactic and an extralinguistic context. This makes it possible for emergentists to look at all kinds of word learning from the same unbiased perspective: it is not assumed that learning words belonging to one word class must be very different from learning words belonging to another word class. Which words are easy or difficult to learn, or which cues are used by the language learner to find out the meaning of a word, can be different for words within the same word class, but also similar across word classes.

This essay, which will be focusing on the psychological processes involved in learning the meaning of nouns and verbs will be based entirely on books and articles representing the emergentist/constructivist approach. Especially, for the part on learning nouns, an emergentist model called *The Emergentist Coalition Model*, developed and described by George Hollich, Kathy Hirsh-Pasek and Roberta Michnick Golinkoff (2000), will stand in the focus. It regards early word learning as a process of incremental knowledge construction, where each step on this path changes or reshapes the child's cognitive system and provides it with new equipment for the task of further word learning. The second part, dealing with the acquisition of verbs, is based primarily on texts by Ewa Dabrowska (2009) and Gilette et al. (1999), which treat word learning cross-categorically, focusing on properties of words beyond the category level, especially their concreteness, imageability and their semantic and syntactic properties.

Finally, some suggestions will be made as to how the psycholinguistic insights presented so far can be put to use in school, in service of second language teaching.

2. Basic theoretical reflections

In the beginning, when we try to make sense of the process of (first) language acquisition in children, we'll be confronted with the observation that, apparently, humans are the only species which has language. Though children certainly won't be so sure about that, it seems to be the verdict spoken by "serious" science. So, we're told that only humans can use language *symbolically*, whereas other animals only use signs in an *indexical* way (Golinkoff & Hirsh-Pasek, 2000, pp. 8-10). The former means that we're conscious of words or other *symbols* as "standing for" some idea or mental content, i.e. that they're *intentional* in character, whereas the latter signifies that a sign is used as a trigger to induce some kind of reaction, i.e. some instinctive or conditioned behaviour. So, a loud bang will probably cause most animals to run away, or children to cry, creating the impression of danger or abnormal situation. In contrast, when we listen to a speech act performed by some other person, we know that the person uses words to refer to objects, events or ideas, and an automatic reaction on our part is normally inhibited, or, at least, suspended. We then represent mentally the content of what has been conveyed to us and can then respond to this message either by producing a responsive utterance ourselves or by other kinds of behaviour, or by consciously refusing to do anything.

When we (as psycholinguists) accept that humans are the only species who can behave like this, we're left with the obligation to explain the cause of this difference. The most frequent answer, considering our current state of knowledge in biology, has been that there must be some inborn or hereditary mechanism which enables humans to acquire and use (symbolic) language (Pinker, 1994, pp. 18ff; Bates et al., 1998).

To be sure, our entire physical or biological makeup is determined by our genes somehow, so, it is a simple guess to assume that our motor and cognitive abilities are genetically pre-formed or facilitated in some way as well. The receptive capabilities of our senses certainly have to be pre-established in some way, since it has been proven beyond any doubt that different species have different perceptive capabilities. So, some species may lack, e.g., the visual sense altogether, or have a certain range of perception in that field, etc. The same is true for their motor skills and behavioural characteristics, i.e. how fast they can run, how high they can jump, how skilled they are with their body parts, or which sounds they are able to produce. Given the different bodily characteristics as well as perceptual and motor capabilities of animals and humans, it should not come as a surprise that our linguistic behaviour is not found in the same form in any other species. The way we perceive and process visual, acoustic and other signals, and the abilities we have to produce behaviour are certainly in many ways different from other species, so that the outcome of our socialization process is very likely to be dissimilar from theirs.

The question for the scholar or scientist is, in how far, exactly, and in what sense are the abilities of mature animals or humans pre-determined or pre-wired from the beginning, and how much *learning* and *adaptation* contribute to the "end" state of a grown up or mature individual. Put differently, which aspects or parts of knowledge and behaviour of an individual are pre-programmed, and which can be ascribed to some variable, *constructionist* process of development? Concerning the more specific question of language acquisition and development, the last 30 years have seen a rather intensely fought out battle between proponents of a strong nativist view which proposes to actually do away with the concept of *learning*, being convinced that the steady state of a mature organism with respect to behaviour and cognition is pre-programmed genetically; and the camp of *emergentists* and *constructivists*, who believe that though some *constraints* on development are provided for by the innate tendencies of the human brain to form certain patterns of circuitry – which enhance or enable certain cognitive processes and behaviours –, learning and experience, or self-constructing processes, have to be taken seriously, since they can be accredited a considerable influence on the individual outcome (Bates et al., 1998; Bates, 1999). So, constructivists tend to perhaps overemphasize differences between individuals and their individual trajectories of development, whereas nativists tend to downplay the potential for individual paths of development in human beings, and try to equate learning and development with *maturation,* i.e. a process by which genetically pre-determined properties of the organism at a certain time automatically come into being (Pinker, 1994, pp. 288f). Formulated in a positive way it can be said that constructivists

4

emphasize the active part an individual plays in his/her own development, while nativists remind us of the biologically pre-given paths and limits of learning, which often present themselves as steps and stages in cognitive and linguistic development.

Trying to find some common ground between these two conflicting approaches, it is probably most proper to say that children, when approaching the task of learning/acquiring a language, bring certain predispositions with them which make the task at hand easier or possible in the first place. Except for some individuals who suffer from certain functional disorders, the vast majority of humans is equipped with the ability to perceive or hear all the sounds human languages consist of, to produce these sounds, too, and to process and store them in such a way, that they can be retrieved in parts and be recombined, so as to form novel and meaningful utterances, which are understood by other humans speaking the same language. Though it has been thought long time that this process is more or less completed at the age of four and that this steady state of linguistic competence comprises roughly the same cognitive structures in all healthy individuals, it has been shown more recently that, firstly, the development of grammatical knowledge goes on well into the adulthood, and, secondly, that it is very individual in the particular cognitive structures which underlie performance (Dabrowska, 2008). Consequently, what at the surface may look as comparable knowledge of grammar across individuals, can differ considerably in terms of the cognitive structures which generate the overt behaviours. Still, it can't be denied that typical four years old children can comprehend a vast array of words and sentences and can produce them, too.

3. Biases, Constraints and Cues: The Emergentist Coalition Model (ECM)

The *emergentist coalition model,* formulated by Hirsh-Pasek and Golinkoff (Golinkoff & Hirsh-Pasek, 2000; Hollich, Hirsh-Pasek & Golinkoff, 2000), is characterized by the use of three different basic concepts: *constraints, cues* and *biases.* Each has a separate psychological function, but the three are thought to be highly interdependent.

Several *constraints* have been proposed in the literature to account for the apparent ease with which infants learn new words (Karmiloff & Karmiloff-Smith, 2002, pp. 68-72). The ECM reuses several of the constraints proposed in the literature and integrates them in one model. This model can in so far be regarded as an improvement to the former ideas as it gives the particular constraints, which have previously stood in isolation without any obvious connection to each other, specific temporal and psychological functions within *one* dynamic developmental system (Bloom, 2000, p. 124f). The basic idea here is that the constraints/principles of word learning are the emergent result of previous learning processes, i.e. "they are the products and not the engines of lexical development" (Hirsh-Pasek et al. 2000, p. 146). Thus, the authors of the ECM follow the self-imposed claim not only to describe some learning mechanisms and stages of language proficiency in children but to explain how processes and mechanisms of learning emerge and change over time (Hirsh-Pasek et al. 2000, p. 160; Hollich et al. 2000, p. 111). This shows in the architecture of the model (*figure 1*), where the particular constraints are arranged in two tiers of three constraints each, which are supposed to apply in a temporal order in that the constraints of the second tier can only start their work when the three constraints of the first tier have consecutively been applied.

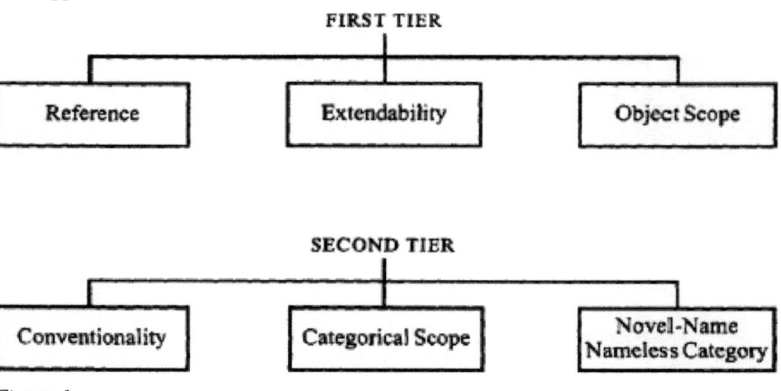

Figure 1

In Addition to the *constraints/principles* the authors use the concept of *cues* as a basic psychological category to explain processes in word learning. A *cue* in this context is a stimulus or perception which helps somebody (in this case the child) to become aware of something, especially in the sense of realizing a relation or connection between different mental contents (like concepts, perceptions etc.). Perhaps we can also call a cue a channel through which a connection between two or more different entities is being realized or established.[1] Although there is certainly a huge variety of cues which can be used by children in the process of acquiring a language, the authors of the ECM speak of three general types of cues which play a prominent role in the process: *perceptual, social* and *linguistic cues* (Hirsh-Pasek et al. 2000). The perceptual cue, which the authors basically equate to *object salience*, concerns the question how easy it is to see or perceive something in the first place. So, object size, shape, colour, distance from the observer are factors which determine the salience of the object. A further factor, which is even of greater importance in the context of establishing new object-word mappings, is the appeal an object has for the child, i.e. whether the child finds the object interesting or attractive, so as to pay attention to it. *Social cues* have to do with the question whether the child is able to use forms of social interaction like pointing to something or eye-gaze to form new object-word mappings. A basic requirement for this to happen would be establishing *joint attention* or some kind of *shared intentionality* between child and the speaker. The third category of *cues* is constituted by *linguistic cues*, i.e. perceived features stemming from areas like morphology and syntax. For example, children learn very early the distributional characteristics of subjects, verbs and objects within a sentence and the typical inflected verb forms like those ending in – *ing* or –*ed* (Karmiloff & Karmiloff-Smith, 2002, p. 73). Hearing a sentence like "Cookie Monster is squatting Big Bird" they can apply the *linguistic cues* to identify a skeletal meaning of the sentence and recognize the right action when given the choice of several different pictures, even if they haven't known the verb 'to squat' before (Hollich et al., p. 109). In conducting experiments with children, the experimenters try to control the accessibility of these cues in order to establish which cues make which learning effects possible. The authors believe that there is a close relationship between cues and constraints in word learning. The basic mechanism of word-to-object mapping, as hypothesised by the authors, is that the utilization of certain cues by the child brings with it the emergence of certain principles, which, in turn, control the word learning process (Hirsh-Pasek et al., p. 146).

The third basic term in the model is *bias*. Though the authors do not devote much space to this idea or concept, it seems to be important for the overall understanding of

---

[1] Since I haven't found any exact definition of the term *cue* in the literature I have used, this is my rendering of the concept, based on how I have understood it from the texts.

the theory. While *cues* and *constraints* are rather explicit constructs which can be described in some detail and be illustrated by examples, *biases* are very vague and can be hardly described at all. They mean something like a *tendency*, without being able to tell exactly what this *tendency* consists of. So, there is probably a bias in human babies to pay a closer attention to human voices than to other sounds. Such biases are hard to tell and the authors don't even try to exactly describe or enumerate them. The point is that they are more basic and less explicit in their function than *constraints/principles* or *cues* are. Their existence, however, allows these later mental tools to come into being (Hollich et al., 2000, p. 113).

3.1 Reference or the semiotic/symbolic function of language

The first of the above six *principles* of language acquisition will be given special attention, since it is by far the most basic and most important one. One can say without exaggeration that the language acquisition/learning process stands and falls with the very ability of humans to treat words as referential or symbolic in nature.

Hirsh-Pasek and Michnick Golinkoff (2000) evoke the distinction between *indexes* and *symbols* to make the specifity of reference, i.e. the use of symbols, clear. Indexes are signs that co-occur in some sense with the object they're related to: So the beep of a microwave is an index for the fact that the process of heating the food is finished; the ringing of the bell indicates that there is someone in front of our door; or the fuel reserve indicator in our car lights up as soon as the amount of fuel in the tank has sunk below a certain level. Thus, you simply can't have the first without the second; they always go hand in hand. On the psychological level, which we're talking about, an indexical relation would amount to some instinctive or conditioned reaction; e.g. as soon as the animal perceives a certain kind of danger it gives a certain kind of cry; or as soon as the antelope sees a lion she runs away to save her life. Transferring this principle to a human situation and language use, we could think of the mother using always the same expression to announce that lunch or dinner is ready, or the child automatically running to the table as soon as it hears these words. But though such co-occurrences of situations and specific language use can certainly happen now and then, according to certain routines, we know that there is a lot of freedom and variety in human communication. We know that communication doesn't just *happen*, reactively –

8

though sometimes it does – but that it is generally adjusted to some purpose, intention or goal, which exists only as an idea or representation in the mind of the speaker. Thus it becomes clear that a truly linguistic human communication is different from purely associative mechanisms that characterize instinctive animal calls or any forms of conditioned behaviour, which would be examples of an *indexical* relation between object or event and the sign that 'goes' with it. When we think of a truly *symbolic* use of language or other signs, we assume that the *signifier* (i.e. the sign) and the *signified* (i.e. the 'thing' which is meant by the use of the sign) can be dissociated from each other and be used deliberately in different situations. This requires the ability on the part of the interlocutors to mentally represent the objects or events they are talking about without these objects or events being present. The participants in a dialogue can talk not only about things which cannot currently be experienced or events that happened long ago, they can even talk about imaginary things like science fiction or fairy tales, their plans for the future or purely subjective topics like the fear of being betrayed by somebody and so on. Obviously, the communication on these topics relies solely on the *imagination* or *cognitive representation* of these things by the persons involved in the discourse. From very early on children have to have the ability to *represent* the content of linguistic expressions in a similar form, otherwise language learning could never "take off the ground" (Hirsh-Pasek et al., p. 139). Thus, it must be assumed that before children attach a sign (linguistic symbol or word) to an object or event, they have to *conceive of* the object or event in some way. So, what children do when they learn to use a word for something, is not attach the word 'to the thing' itself or to the immediate perception of it, because then it couldn't be used in the absence of that thing, but to their own cognitive or mental *representation* of the thing in question. The representation of things, events, mental states of others or ideas is the requirement for forming different types of categories which refer to *concepts* and not to any entities or phenomena that exist as such, independently from their *concepts* or *representations*. Even a seemingly concrete noun like 'clothes' cannot be inferred immediately from the perception of some particular object since a 'clothe' as an instantiation of the corresponding category doesn't exist – it is a group label for socks, shoes, underwear, coats etc. So, already at this level an abstraction or generalization from the concrete sense perception is required in order to learn what the sign/word refers to.

It is one thing, however, to say that the ability to form concepts of things, events and other people's intentions is a requirement for acquiring language and to state that somehow it is there, and another one to give an account of how this ability comes about. A tentative explanation is given by Michnick Golinkoff and Hirsh-Pasek (2000). Following Deacon (1997) they suggest that the *inhibition* of immediate *associations* might be the key to the formation of *symbolic representations*. In order to overcome a simple *indexical* relationship between the object and the sign, the individual has to free himself from the immediate impulse of the association mechanism by deferring the indexical association from the focus of attention. By doing this, a possibility opens up for the individual to search "for relationships at a higher level" and to use a sign "in another, more global, way" (Michnick Golinkoff & Hirsh-Pasek, 2000, p. 7). It is suggested that probably the prefrontal cortex of human brains serves this function of blocking immediate indexical associations between stimulus and response "by entertaining some form of 'not'". Since 'nots' are not given in our sense perceptions they must be understood to "come from meaning", which is "outside the world of the senses" (ibid.).

A very similar suggestion has been made by Kinsbourne (1983) in a slightly different context, however. According to him, it is a property of "more mature" brains to overcome "the innately formed response tendencies" to the most salient stimuli and to move down the "perceptual hierarchy", paying attention to ever less salient stimuli and responding in ways which are ever freer. Eventually, the mature individual reaches the ability to "respond ... to certain arbitrary conjunctions of stimuli with arbitrary response patterns" (Kinsbourne, 1983, p. 152). The 'maturity of brains' seems here to coincide or be identical with the ability to suppress automatic reactions and to respond in arbitrary fashion to given stimuli. Kinsbourne believes that it is a sign or feature of intelligent behaviour to be able to "entertain improbabilities, and to depart from the most familiar response or from attending to the most salient aspect of the situation" (ibid, p. 153/4).

Both of the above accounts support the idea that the ability to refrain from inborn mechanisms can be seen as a basic prerequisite to intelligent non-mechanistic behaviour and therefore also to language learning and language use. This view forms a stark contrast to the ideas proposed by generative grammarians and other proponents of the idea of innate forms of knowledge, by suggesting that the absence from or resistance to specialized cognitive and behavioural mechanisms rather than obedience to them forms the basis of the uniquely human intelligent capabilities. The symbolic use of language certainly is one such typically human skill, whose sophistication is probably better explained in terms of inhibition of innately specified response strategies than in terms of their utilization.[2]

In any case, human communication cannot be thought of without the principle of reference or symbolic use of language. Only when we understand that someone else is speaking about his perceptions, intentions or ideas are we in a position to react sensibly, to give some answer etc. It is only because of shared concepts respectively common symbolic representations that stand behind or are tied to linguistic expressions that human communication makes sense (Enfield, 2000, p. 36).

3.2 Other principles of the ECM

After this relatively exhaustive treatment of the topic of *reference* and *symbol use*, we now turn to the other constraints on word learning proposed in the *emergentist coalition model*.

The principle of *extendibility* suggests that words usually do not refer to particular objects but can be used to refer to other similar objects as well. What this 'similarity' is based on, however, cannot be generalized across individuals (Hollich et al. 2000, p.6). Some children extend words based on shape, some on colour or some on smell. It is only some time later, with the application of a still different constraint, which Hollich et al. call *the categorical scope*, that children learn to use words 'properly', i.e. as is required by their language community. It seems to be the case, however, that there is a general bias or tendency in children to use shape as the basis for word extension (ibid.). It has been also suggested that the *extendibility* principle is used by children as young as 12 months.

The third constraint on the first tier is called *object scope*. It encompasses two elements that can be found elsewhere in the literature: the *whole object assumption* and the preference to name *objects* before *actions* (Hirsh-Pasek et al., 2000, p. 139/140) The first of these two principles stipulates that the child will assume a word refers to a whole object rather than its parts or some particular attributes like colour or smell. The second part simply says that children are more ready to suppose that a word stands for an object rather than for an action.

---

[2] For a broad discussion of the idea that the increasingly elaborate use of signs (semiosis) by higher organisms may be read as an indicator of their greater freedom of behaviour, see Hoffmeyer (2010).

It has been suggested that the three principles mentioned above operate as early as in the first year of life. By then acquisition of new words is a tedious and slow process. At the age of roughly 12 months children possess a passive vocabulary of 30 items. One year later, however, the child will be able to *actively* use ten times as many words and to learn 8 to 9 new words every day! So, what happens in between? It seems that some major change in the cognitive processes responsible for word learning must have occurred. Hirsh-Pasek et al. suggest that there is a shift in the child's attentional focus and the emergence of new constraints that regulate the learning process. Attention is believed to be a basic factor in the word learning process. Only when a child's attention is directed towards the object and the corresponding sign (word) is clearly perceptible for the child can the reference relation between the two be established. But, attention – or the child's consciousness – is only a general disposition; it has to use certain cognitive paths in order to be successful. These further cognitive paths the child utilizes in the language learning process in her second year of life are grouped on the second tier in the *emergentist coalition model*. This encompasses the *conventionality,* the *categorical scope*, and the *novel-name/nameless category* principles.

Conventionality can best be understood when we consider that children who have already mastered the *reference* principle often invent idiosyncratic words of their own to label objects or events in their environment. *Conventionality* then just says that children in the second year of life increasingly give up their own word creations since they become conscious that they have to use words that are also used by others in order to be understood.

The principle of *categorical scope* rests on and is an evolution of the *extendibility* principle. But whereas extendibility only prompts the child to use a word elsewhere, outside the context of its original occurrence, the categorical scope principle stipulates that children become able to conceive of word referents as categories of things. These categories have to be learned according to the conventions of the community of speakers. That this is not anything which is inborn or comes 'as if from above' can be seen through the many 'errors' children tend to make in naming objects before they learn the defining features on the basis of which a word label may be extended (Karmiloff-Smith, 2002, p.66-67).

Finally, the *novel-name/nameless category* principle helps the child with the word learning process by prompting her to map a novel word onto a category for which she doesn't have a label yet. So, by hearing a new word, children will assume that it must refer to an object they don't have a name for yet and bring the two candidates together.

3.3 Results of the ECM studies

The ECM is a comprehensive groundwork for research in language acquisition, which, as the authors themselves concede, is far from being complete. It is intended to serve as a fundament for further research in the field of word/language learning or acquisition. The basic ingredient of this theory is its clearly developmental orientation, the tenet of taking learning and development seriously, i.e. even though some natural predisposition of humans to embark on certain trajectories of development are accepted, the emphasis is put on studying and *explaining process and change* over time rather than on *describing states and stages* (Hirsh-Pasek et al., 2000, p.161). Thus, explaining process and change of language learning over developmental time is the goal of this approach.

What has been achieved so far is basically some insight into the process of word learning that seems to significantly change in character from the first to the second, to third year of life. As the authors explain, the acquisition process is very slow and laborious in the beginning, i.e. in the first year of life (Hollich et al., 2000, p. 1). Then, some time around the 18th or 19th month, most children experience a *vocabulary spurt*. From then on, they become able to learn 8 to 10 words every day, instead of just 1 or two per weak, as was the case some months before. This sudden change in word learning efficiency must certainly have a basis in a change of the psychological mechanisms that underlie the learning process, as the authors conclude (...). Supported by the experiments they have conducted, they ascribe this shift primarily to the emergence of a stable adult-like principle of reference around the end of the second year. Children then primarily rely on the subtle social cue of *eye-gaze* to relate words uttered by a speaker to things or events in the environment (Hirsh-Pasek et al., 2000, p. 158). The most potent characterization of this shift suggests that while the word learning process in children before the emergence of the mature reference principle is based on associative attentional mechanisms, it then becomes controlled by the fuller awareness of the referential function of words and language (Hollich et al., 2000, p. 110-111). These distinct strategies of learning show in experiments as distinctive use of cues in word learning tasks. 1-year-olds needed the convergence of multiple cues (they had to be *salient*, i.e. interesting for the child; they were looked at and even handled by the experimenter) plus much time and many repetitions of the object presentations for word learning to take place. For 24-month-olds, however, it was enough to follow the speaker's eye-gaze to conclude which object was being talked about and they easily learned the word that belonged to it.

A second important change in children's word learning abilities is the shift from a mere *extension* of words to different objects to the emergence of a *categorical scope* for extending words. Thus, whereas children do start very early to extend particular words to different objects, they often do this on the basis of some idiosyncratic non-conventional criteria such as shape, colour or some other kind of similarity (Hollich et al., 2000, p. 106/7). They do not yet fully grasp what the basis for extension actually is. It is only after they have had some experience with the objects and have won a deeper understanding of their properties and function that the conventional *categorical scope* for extension emerges.

Though some further minor aspects of development have been mentioned in the volumes under review, these summaries should suffice to give a picture of the most important results obtained through the application of the model. But whereas here we were almost exclusively concerned with the learning of common nouns, the next chapter will be focusing on verbs.

4. Learning Verbs

So far we have been concerned with the acquisition of nouns and with concrete common nouns at that. There is considerable consensus in the literature that verbs are harder to learn than verbs (Gillette et al., 1999, p. 137). And indeed, it can even easily occur to an attentive thinker that it is not as easy to say when an activity starts and when it ends, and therefore to realize what the essence of a particular activity is, as it is to look at an object, take it in one's hand and cognitively grasp its essence or identity. And this is just the beginning. In the same way as there are abstract nouns that denote entities which can't be touched or seen, there are a great many verbs that stand for activities which exist only as ideas in the mind of the speaker and have no equivalent in the external world, e.g. 'consider', 'suppose' etc. Besides, this difficulty is not restricted to mental verbs like the examples in the preceding sentence. One can easily think of other verbs like 'converge', 'deviate' or 'enable', which don't denote any particular activities, not even mental ones, but relate somehow to unspecified processes in a very general way. Ewa Dabrowska (2009) introduces a distinction between *basic* and *non-basic* vocabulary to bring into focus the disparities which exist between words regarding their concreteness or relatedness to extralinguistic contexts. By *basic* vocabulary she means "words designating relatively concrete entities which are learned early in development in the context of face-to-face interaction, where the extralinguistic context offers a rich source of information about meaning" (Dabrowska 2009, p. 201). What is specific about *basic* vocabulary, according to her view, is that they can somewhat clearly be related to the extralinguistic, visible reality. 'The cat sat on the mat' would be an example of such a rather basic vocabulary use, given that the situation described by the sentence has been experienced by the learner. In such rather simple cases the learners can make use of many "situational clues" which help them establish the meaning of the words that have been used (ibid.). By contrast, the category of *non-basic* vocabulary comprises the many expressions that are either designating abstract concepts like those cited above or words which, although referring to perceptible phenomena, are very rarely used in face-to-face verbal interaction. Such words, like 'scurry', 'ogle' or 'capacious' are primarily used in written texts (ibid.). Thus, a young child beginning to learn her first language hardly ever comes across such expressions. It seems therefore that such *difficult* vocabulary may be difficult for two different reasons: firstly, because the linguistic input cannot be compared to any 'real', physical context; and secondly, because some expressions are so rarely used that they hardly occur in informal conversation. What is especially interesting about these words is that they predominantly appear in some specific semantic context and show a co-occurrence with other particular words or expressions. Thus their range of use is tied to a narrow semantic field and their appearance can be predicted by the other words which frequently co-occur with them in a sentence (collocations). According to Dabrowska, "a word's collocations and semantic preferences" are "the single most important source of information that learners use to learn relational words from linguistic context" (ibid, p. 206).

Very similar ideas have been expressed by Gillette (1999). Beginning with the observation that nouns preponderate in the vocabulary of infants in their first three years of life, she attends to the question why verbs appear to be so much harder for children to learn. She formulates the hypothesis that, in general, extralinguistic information may not be enough to learn verbs and that identification of verbs in the input may require the additional "inspection of their standard *linguistic contexts* of use" (ibid, p. 138). She then goes on about verifying this hypothesis in three experiments. The first one is a simulation of word learning with adults (college students). These were shown videotaped scenes of mothers engaged in play with their children. The subjects were asked to guess which words the mothers used in particular moments of the scenes shown. The sound was not available to the subjects. The result was that the participants could rightly guess the involved nouns in 45 percent of the cases. The score for the verbs, even though these were basic words like 'come', 'do' or 'make', was only 15 percent. This outcome has shown that verbs are generally much more difficult to be linked with the extralinguistic reality than are nouns. What was perhaps even more striking, however, was the broad variability range for the number of correct answers, since 28 subjects were tested on each particular word. So, as for the verbs, eight of them (out of 24) could not be conjectured by any of the 28 subjects (think, know, make, like, love, pop, say, have), whereas one particular verb (throw) was rightly conjectured by 86% of the subjects! Besides, rather easy to conjecture were the verbs 'come' (75%), 'look' (42.9%), 'push' (42.9%) and 'put' (35,9%). This result has led the authors straightforward to the question how one could account for these obvious differences in the degrees of 'conjectureability' of these words, and therefore probably of their learnability. A suggested answer for this enigma has been that some kind of "concreteness" or "imageability" had to be responsible for the relative easiness with which particular words could be guessed or conjectured. This would also partly explain why "young children's vocabularies are heavily loaded with 'concrete' and 'picturable' words and thin on 'abstract' ones" (ibid, p. 150). In a further experiment Gilette et al. therefore had the words rated by subjects for their *imageability*. Imageability "seems to reflect most simply the hypothetical distinction between words that can be learned by viewing their instances and those that cannot" (ibid, p. 151). In this experiment subjects were asked to rate the imageability of the 48 words (24 nouns and 24 verbs) which were used in the first experiment on a scale from 1 to 7. To get an idea of what *imageability* is supposed to stand for, the subjects were told that a "high imagery rating" should be given to a "word which, in your estimation, arouses a mental image (i.e. a mental picture … or other sensory experience) very quickly and easily" (ibid). As examples for such high imagery words 'sweet' and 'above' were specified; examples of low imagery were 'ambitious' and 'of'. As had been expected, verbs were generally given a much lower imagery rate than nouns. When rated on the same single scale, the mean rating for nouns was 6.08 and for verbs 3.59. Especially, there was only one verb, 'to hammer' (rated 5.56), that came close to the mean value for nouns. In a further step Gilette et al. investigated whether there is any significant correlation between imageability ratings and the results of the previous identifiability/conjecture experiment. And indeed, the correlation between the two properties of verbs has been found as statistically very high ($r = 0.43$). The rather straightforward conclusion the authors have come to regarding these findings has been that "only observables – the most 'pictureable' or 'imageable' items – can be efficiently acquired by observation operating alone" (ibid, p. 153). They further state that "this shows up as a massive advantage for nouns over verbs in the early vocabulary of children" (ibid). Consequently, children's early 'preference' for (concrete) nouns is best explained in terms of the availability of the required information, i.e. the observable referents that go with them. On the flip side, it turns out that observation and reliance on extralinguistic, physical reality "is an inefficient and errorful basis for most word learning beyond the animal noises and concrete basic-level nomimals" (ibid). But, what has also been concluded is that what at a first glance appeared to be a *category* effect, i.e. the prerogative of being a noun or a verb in relation to word learning outcomes, is better explained in terms of the *imageability* of particular items, be they nouns or verbs (ibid, p. 149).

As a next step the researchers have conducted a comprehensive experiment consisting of six rather distinct experimental settings or conditions. As in the first experiment, the participants – 20 college students for each setting – were to guess or conjecture which verbs were uttered by mothers to their babies, but they were given very different material (cues) for this task. Some were only allowed to look at the silent video, with beeps marking the verbs; others were given lists with nouns which co-occurred with the verbs in a sentence; still others were given some syntactic information (prepositions and auxiliaries were provided in the right places) and some were provided with combinations of videos and varying degrees of linguistic information. As it has turned out, syntactic or additional lexical information (the words co-occurring in the sentence) was much more helpful in finding the target verb than a visual presentation of the scene (video). When presented only a syntactic frame consisting of prepositions and modals/auxiliaries, plus nonce words as placeholders, the subjects correctly conjectured the sought for verb in 52% of the cases! When the syntactic cues were missing, but the participants were shown the scene on video instead, the score was only 29%. Though, as the authors themselves concede, these experiments cannot be taken to directly represent the word learning situation of children, they strongly suggest that for learning verbs the linguistic (syntactic, lexical) context is much more helpful than any extralinguistic physical or social environment!

In sum, the experiments conducted by Gillette et al. consistently suggest an entire line of linguistic development. At first, concrete or 'picturable' nouns and verbs are learned. After a basic stock of such words has been acquired, the knowledge of grammar grows, since enough building blocks have become available in order to build larger linguistic structures. Then, in turn, knowledge of grammar helps the infant to find out the meaning of words which, though low on the imagery scale, begin to make sense in a linguistic context which provides rich grammatical and semantic cues for decoding their meaning.

The cross-categorical nature of word semantics (or rather the psychological mechanisms which produce semantic representations) suggested by the authors due to the outcomes of their experiments, is clearly supported by another study, conducted by Bird et al. (2000). Bird et al. have investigated the question of grammatical category effects on word processing by studying aphasic patients who had difficulties with word access or production. These patients have apparently shown category specific deficits when tested on naming tasks. After extensive tests with patients, other test persons and computer simulations, and after reviewing relevant literature on the issue, the authors have come to the conclusion that what often appears to be a category effect in word processing is more parsimoniously explained in terms of accessibility of different semantic features in a *semantic space* (ibid, p. 256). This semantic space can be best described as a coordinate system with (at least) two axes: one axis indicating the richness of *sensory* features (like shape, colour or smell), the other indicating the abundance of *functional* features (what can be done with it?) (*figure 2*). What has been considered a rather enigmatic case before – people who had a deficit in the production of nouns referring to animate objects, but who were spared at 'inanimates' and verbs – could be explained rather straightforwardly with this model. Thus, animate nouns were found to possess more sensory features than inanimate nouns or verbs. 'Inanimates' and verbs, in contrast, are richer in functional than sensory features.

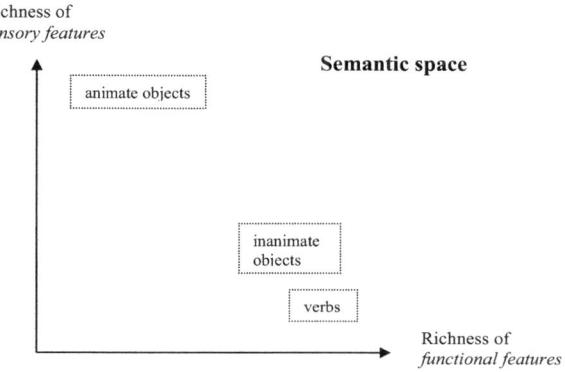

Richness of
sensory features

Semantic space

animate objects

inanimate objects

verbs

Richness of
functional features

Figure 2

The theory could thus explain the test results elegantly by appealing to the idea of a unitary *semantic space* instead of relying on the conventional concept of *categories*, which are often thought to have some fundamental 'biological' status. This finding is also more in line with the emergentist/constructivist approaches to the study of language, which view grammatical categories as the outcome of usage and a function of the context of use rather than some ontological given (Broccias, 2013).

The above articles by Dabrowska, Bird et al. and Gillette et al. have painted a rather coherent picture of word learning and processing. This picture also reveals the kind of continuity that probably exists between early word learning in young children and learning in adolescents or even adults. Especially the experiments conducted by Gillette et al. show the peculiar effects of different cues on 'conjecturing' the meaning of words. These experiments, though realized with adult participants, seem to be extremely telling for first language acquisition as well. They are the best evidence that there might not be any substantial difference between first and second acquisition at all (cf. Ellis, 2006).

5. Conclusions for second language teaching at school

Though the processes described so far were primarily related to word learning in infants who were at the stage of acquiring their first language, it is certainly not inconsistent or irrational to use these insights in second language learning classroom. First of all, we were concerned here with the learning of words, so the hypotheses of generative grammar concerning innate knowledge of language and the workings of *universal grammar*, and hence the putative *critical period hypothesis*, cannot be successfully applied here, since even the supporters of these theories concede that the content of word meaning must be learned from the input. From the point of view of constructivist or emergentist, developmentally oriented theories, the question of relevance of first to second language learning doesn't arise at all, since all psychological development is regarded as a continuous, life-long self regulating process, where each step is interrelated and interconnected with all other steps before and after (MacWhinney, 1998). First language acquisition appears here therefore as the basis of an "incremental learning machinery" (Gilette et al. 1999, p. 154) which grows and gains momentum with development. So, understanding the very first steps of this "incremental learning" process is crucial to understanding any further development. For a teacher to look separately at second language learners and apply blindly pre-formulated rules for teaching would seem very dubious from the very beginning.

Still, some basic precepts regarding second language teaching in class can be inferred from these results. We have seen that what we may call *basic vocabulary*, i.e. highly imagery words like concrete nouns and verbs like 'push' or 'throw', is learnable from the participation in a semantically rich physical context, full of objects and stimulating diverse activities. Though basically such conditions are not easily available at school, objects and pictures as well as videos can provide some of the stimuli and cues required. Outside activities and excursions may further provide the basis for learning basic nouns and verbs. As for the more 'advanced' non-basic vocabulary, learning anyway primarily occurs as a result of the exposition to (written or spoken) texts. Here classical reading and text exercises will do their job, but perhaps even better is the contact with spoken language through audio books or recordings and especially films. Films not only offer the learner the full range of (everyday) discourse but also the visual cues that form the extralinguistic context for the language used.

What seems to make only very little sense with regard to learning *non-basic* vocabulary, is the learning of isolated words from lists, as is often done at schools. As has been pointed out, for this type of vocabulary it is not so much the translatable meaning that tells one how to properly use the word, but its position within a syntactic frame and the co-occurrence of its typical collocations.

6. Conclusion

The learning of a language certainly is something of a big mystery, which can't be unveiled by offering simple explanations consisting of a handful causes or constraints. In an emergentist approach it is best viewed as a slow and incremental process with some sudden spurts now and then, depending on the accumulation effect of acquired skills and knowledge.

It seems that the emergence of the *reference principle* in children, which probably shows up at the end of the first year, is a turning point in the process of language acquisition and the development of linguistic knowledge. From now on children stop to blindly associate sound patterns with the perception of objects and consciously treat human utterances as fulfilling an intentional function, i.e. as having meaning. They can then guess or conjecture the mental states of others using several kinds of cues in the environment and the behaviour of the persons involved. Even though, they will start learning the words or utterances that can be inferred from the perceptible, physical environment in which the encountered speech acts are embedded. Thus, only 'picturable' nouns and verbs like those referring to concrete objects and visible activities will be learned at this stage. Later on, when a basic stock of nouns and verbs has been acquired, the child becomes able to increasingly integrate grammatical knowledge into her linguistic competence. At even later stages, when a considerable knowledge of grammatical schemas and typical collocation patterns for many different words has been acquired, the child learns ever more abstract and rare words and becomes ever more fluent and efficient in the use of this astonishing instrument called language.

The emergentist/constructivist approaches to the study of language don't make much of a difference between (first) language acquisition and (second) language learning. Both are seen as basically the same kind of cognitive process, which is based on general cognitive mechanisms. Generally, not even a categorical distinction between learning/acquiring nouns or verbs is being made, but an apparent distinction between these categories is explained in terms of other general cognitive features that may be more typical for one word class than the other.

Based on the theories reviewed in this paper, some basic recommendations as to the organization of teaching a second language at school can be given. These would favour semantically rich, 'realistic' settings, involving many different objects and activities, for acquiring basic level vocabulary consisting primarily of concrete common nouns and 'picturable' verbs referring to practical activities. For learning non-basic vocabulary, consisting of abstract, very specific or rare words, the use of written or spoken texts (recordings, including films) is unavoidable and must stand at the forefront of teaching in class.

Literature

Bates, Elizabeth et al. (1998): Innateness and Emergentism. In: Bechtel, William & Graham, George (Eds.): A Companion to Cognitive Science. Oxford: Blackwell.

Bates, Elizabeth (1999): Language and the infant brain. In: *Journal of Communication Disorders*, Vol. 32/4, 195-205.

Bird, Helen; Howard, David; Franklin, Sue (2000): Why is a verb like an inanimate object? Grammatical category and semantic category deficits. In: *Brain and Language*, Vol. 72, 246-309.

Bloom, Lois (2000): Pushing the limits on theories of word learning. In: *Monographs of the Society for Research in Child Development,* Vol. 65/3, 124-135.

Broccias, Cristiano (2013): Cognitive Grammar. In: Hoffmann, Thomas & Trousdale, Graeme (Eds.): The Oxford Handbook of Construction Grammar. Oxford: OUP.

Bybee, Joan & McClelland, James (2007): Gradience of gradience: a reply to Jackendoff. In: *Linguistic Review*, Vol. 24, 436-455.

Dabrowska, Ewa (2008): The later development of an early-emerging system: the curious case of the Polish genitive. In: *Linguistics*, Vol. 46/3, 629-650.

Dabrowska, Ewa (2009): Words as Constructions. In: Pourcel, Stephanie & Evans, Vyvyan (Eds.): New Directions in Cognitive Linguistics. Amsterdam: Benjamins.

Ellis, Nick (1998): Emergentism, connectionism and language learning. In: *Language Learning,* Vol. 48/4, 631-664.

Ellis, Nick (2006): Language acquisition as rational contingency learning. In: *Applied Linguistics*, Vol. 27/1, 1-24.

Enfield, Nick (2000): The theory of Cultural Logic. How individuals combine social intelligence with semiotics to create cultural meaning. In: *Cultural Dynamics*, Vol. 12/1, 35-64.

Gillette, Jane et al. (1999): Human simulations of vocabulary learning. In: *Cognition*, Vol. 73, 135-176.

Golinkoff, Roberta & Hirsh-Pasek, Kathryn (2000): Word learning. Icon, index or symbol? In: Golinkoff, R. & Hirsh-Pasek, K. (Eds.): Becoming a Word Learner: A Debate on Lexical Acquisition, Oxford: OUP.

Hirsh-Pasek, Kathryn; Golinkoff, Roberta; Hollich, George (2000): An Emergentist Coalition Model for word learning. In: Golinkoff, R. & Hirsh-Pasek, K. (Eds.): Becoming a Word Learner: A Debate on Lexical Acquisition. Oxford: OUP.

Hoffmeyer, Jesper: God and the World of Signs: Semiotics and the Emergence of Life. In: *Zygon*, Vol. 45/2, 367-390.

Hollich, George; Hirsh-Pasek, Kathryn; Golinkoff, Roberta (2000): Breaking the language barrier. An Emergentist Coalition Model of word learning. In: *Monographs of the Society for Research in Child Development*, Vol. 65/3.

Karmiloff, Kyra & Karmiloff-Smith, Annette (2002): Pathways to Language: From Fetus to Adolescent. Cambridge, MA: Harvard UP.

Kinsbourne, Marcel & Rieber, Robert (1983): Marcel Kinsbourne's views on the psychology of language and thought. In: Rieber, Robert (Ed.): Dialogues on the Psychology of Language and Thought. Conversations with Noam Chomsky, Charles Osgood, Jean Piaget and Marcel Kinsbourne. New York: Plenum.

MacWhinney, Brian (2006): Emergentism – Use Often and With Care. In: *Applied Linguistics*, Vol. 27/4, 729-740.

MacWhinney, Brian (2008): A Unified Model. In: Ellis, Nick & Robinson, Peter (Eds.): Handbook of Cognitive Linguistics and Second Language Acquisition. Erlbaum, Mahwah.

Maguire, Mandy; Hirsh-Pasek, Kathryn; Golinkoff, Roberta (2006): A unified theory of word learning. Putting verb acquisition in context. In: Hirsh-Pasek & Golinkoff (Eds.): Action Meets Word: How Children Learn Verbs. Oxford: OUP.

Pinker, Steven (1994): The Language Instinct. The New Science of Language and Mind. London: Penguin.

Radford, Andrew (2004): Minimalist Syntax. Exploring the Structure of English. Cambridge: CUP.

Verspoor, Marjolyn & Dirven, Rene (2004): Cognitive Exploration of Language and Linguistics. Amsterdam: Benjamins.

YOUR KNOWLEDGE HAS VALUE

- We will publish your bachelor's and
  master's thesis, essays and papers

- Your own eBook and book -
  sold worldwide in all relevant shops

- Earn money with each sale

Upload your text at www.GRIN.com
and publish for free